Faith vs Fear
The Constant Daily Battle That Lives Within Us

Eric J. Singleton

Emerge Publishing Group, LLC
Riviera Beach, FL
www.emergepublishers.com
561.601.0349

© 2014 Eric J. Singleton
All rights reserved.

ISBN: 978-0-9837566-2-0

No part of this book may be reproduced
or transmitted in any form or by any means,
electronic or mechanical without written
permission from the author.

Published by
Emerge Publishing Group LLC
Riviera Beach, FL
www.emergepublishers.com
561-601-0349

Faith vs Fear   Eric J. Singleton
1. Spiritual   2. Biographical

Printed in the United States of America

The purpose of this book is to show, urge, and hopefully inspire Christians, non-Christians and prayerfully non-believers to understand that the Holy Bible is the true and only guide to living life pleasing in God's sight.

~ Eric J. Singleton

Dedication

This book is written and dedicated to my wife Donna M. Singleton whom I love and have been married to for over 28 years; to our children who are all adults, Andre, Quintin, Bryan and Erica; and to our grandchildren.

Inspiration to write this book came from our parents, our families, and our spiritual family. I wrote this book because, I, like so many millions of people of all races, ages, sexes, Christians, and non-Christians, have been living a life of quiet desperation.

Special Thanks
from the Author and Illustrator

I would never have completed this book without the support and inspiration of my lovely wife Donna; thank you. I would also like to say thank you to the Jubar's: Harry and Pamela; thank you to Harry for your support and thank you Pamela for editing my work.

~ Eric J. Singleton

Table of Contents

Worldly Prosperity . . . **3**

Trust God's Way for Your Finances . . . **9**

Working Without Faith . . . **15**

Even God Rested on the Seventh Day . . . **21**

It Takes a Village to Raise a Child . . . **27**

Thank God Justice Prevailed . . . **33**

My Humble Cry Was Heard . . . **45**

Traveling Grace . . . **59**

Humbling Periods and Growing Pains . . . **71**

Call on the Healer First, Then Call the Doctor Second . . . **91**

WORLDLY PROSPERITY

ERIC J. SINGLETON

"Love not the world, neither the things that are in the world. If any man love the world, the love of the Father is not in him."

John 2:15

Chapter 1

Trying to measure up to the world's standards of what success is for many have become a way of life.

The biggest house, the most expensive cars; the latest fads in clothes, shoes, bags, jewelry, the nicest vacations, etc., are all man's view of wealth and prosperity.

I am one of the first to say that having all those things are great achievements as long as you have those things and those things don't have you.

God's word says in 1 John 2:15, *"Love not the world, neither the things that are in the world. If any man love the world, the love of the Father is not in him."*

These very same achievements without God's divine touch on your heart will eventually lead to greed, selfishness, destruction and even fear; especially, if you are financially struggling to pay for and hold on to them.

God's word, II Corinthians 5:7, states *"For we walk by faith, not by sight."* It may be health issues; it may be a social acceptance, but God's word,

Psalm 34:6 states: *"This poor man cried, and the Lord heard him, and saved him out of all his troubles."*

Some people believe in luck or being lucky or unlucky, but for true Christian believers there is no such thing. God is in control of all things. Matthew 7:7, *"Ask, and it shall be given you; seek, and ye shall find; knock, and it shall be opened unto you."* Matthew 7:8, *"For every one that asketh receiveth; and he that seeketh findeth; and to him that knocketh it shall be opened."*

"Ask, and it shall be given you; seek, and ye shall find; knock, and it shall be opened unto you. For every one that asketh receiveth; and he that seeketh findeth; and to him that knocketh it shall be opened."

Matthew 7:7-8

TRUST GOD'S WAY FOR YOUR FINANCES

ERIC J. SINGLETON

"A wise man will hear, and will increase learning; and a man of understanding shall attain unto wise counsels."

Proverbs 1:5

Chapter 2

Only spending time with God when our backs are against the wall and we have tried everything we can think of doing our way without God, we then begin to add Him into the equation.

James 1:5 clearly states, *"If any of you lack wisdom, let him ask of God, that giveth to all men liberally, and upbraideth not; and it shall be given him."*

There are very few adults in any non-dictatorship countries that are total victims of where they are financially, spiritually or any other way in life.

As with anything, there are a few exceptions, but most of us did not plan well enough, followed the wrong leadership or ignored the right leadership. However, it is never too late to make a change. Proverbs 1:5, *"A wise man will hear, and will increase learning; and a man of understanding shall attain unto wise counsels."*

Proverbs 10:14, *"Wise men lay up knowledge: but the mouth of the foolish is near destruction."*

I love my parents and siblings. We have always been a very close family, so close that my father, brother and I worked together in the family business. This business was founded by my father, which was operated in New York for many years.

In 1976, we all moved from New York to Charleston, SC. This is home for both of my parents. When we relocated, the family business was also relocated to Charleston, SC.

After graduating high school in South Carolina, I attended a technical college majoring in Architectural Engineering. I was hired at an engineering firm as a detail draftsman. A year later my father offered me a job in the family business paying more money. I was chasing the dollar trusting man for my finances instead of following the Lord and trusting God for my finances.

II Chronicles 26:5 says, *"...and as long as he sought the Lord, God made him to prosper."*

WORKING WITHOUT FAITH

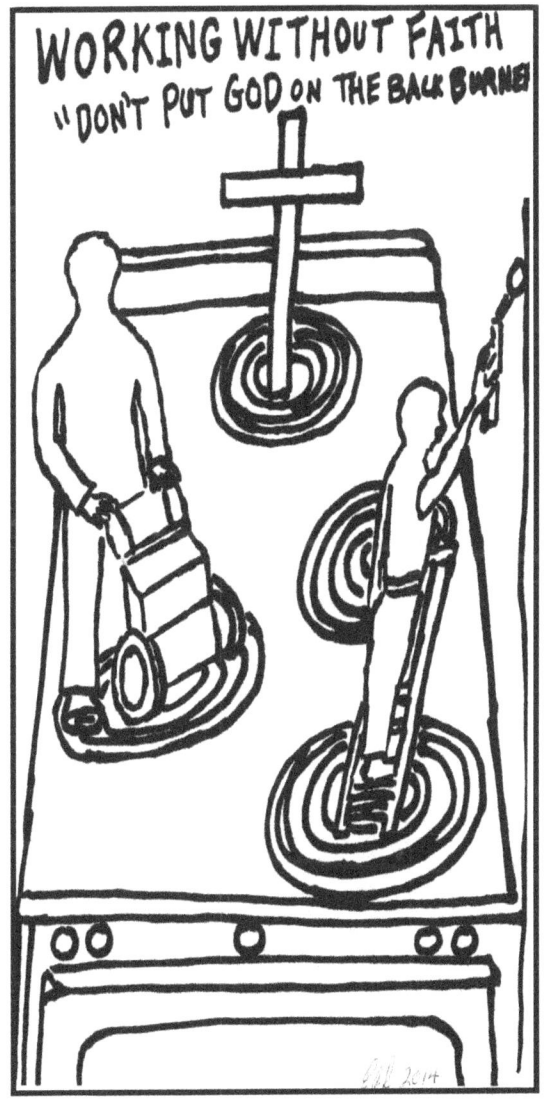

ERIC J. SINGLETON

"Whoso findeth a wife findeth a good thing, and obtaineth favour of the Lord."

Proverbs 18:22

Chapter 3

Philippians 4:13, *"I can do all things through Christ which strengtheneth me."*

Most of us Christians as well as non-Christians are in a constant battle with faith or the lack of faith versus fear.

Often times we lose faith when we take our eyes off God, which is faith and put our eyes on the world, which is by sight.

Faith versus fear is something that we all battle with, some more than others; some everyday and some several times a day.

Faith = Father Always in Thy Heart versus Fear = false evidence appearing real.

At the age of 26 I met a young lady. We dated and after eleven months we got married. Proverbs 18:22, *"Whoso findeth a wife findeth a good thing, and obtaineth favour of the Lord."*

While in my late twenties, married only a few years, my wife and I had small children. At the time I believed in God like most people but I was not saved. And like a lot of believers today, I doubted God's power, presence and control.

I did believe that faith without work is dead, but I believed a lot more that if it is to be it is up to me. So I worked 9-10 hours a day, 5-6 days a week in the family business.

The family business was a moving and storage company handling goods for both military and civilian families as well as office furniture. In addition to this, my wife and I were building a multi-level marketing business in the evening. We also had a paper route; we did the route seven days a week, delivering the newspapers between the hours of 2-5 a.m. We certainly were putting in the work, getting little rest but our faith was in our ability to perform.

EVEN GOD RESTED ON THE SEVENTH DAY

ERIC J. SINGLETON

"Cast thy burden upon the Lord, and he shall sustain thee: he shall never suffer the righteous to be moved."

Psalm 55:22

EVEN GOD RESTED ON THE SEVENTH DAY

★ Chapter 4 ★

Genesis 2:2, *"And on the seventh day God ended his work which he had made; and he rested on the seventh day from all his work which he had made."*

I knew of that scripture back then but I did not follow that because I thought I was getting ahead financially but on Saturday, December 10, 1988 at

12:00 noon one half mile from home I fell asleep behind the wheel. My car crossed the solid line on a single lane highway and hit a bus head on.

In and out of consciousness, I thought I had died and gone to heaven; white clouds, slow motion and talking to the Lord with many regrets. God spared my life. I regained conscious. My face was cut very badly in several places. God not only spared my life but I made a 100% recovery. I walked out of the hospital some five hours later after having cosmetic surgery. I thanked God and a few days later I went back to the same routine for many, many years still not putting God first, and carrying the financial burdens of supporting a family.

EVEN GOD RESTED ON THE SEVENTH DAY

Psalm 55:22 says, *"Cast thy burden upon the Lord, and he shall sustain thee: he shall never suffer the righteous to be moved."*

Now, it is time to put these burdens in God's hand.

"And on the seventh day God ended his work which he had made; and he rested on the seventh day from all his work which he had made."

Genesis 2:2

IT TAKES A VILLAGE TO RAISE A CHILD

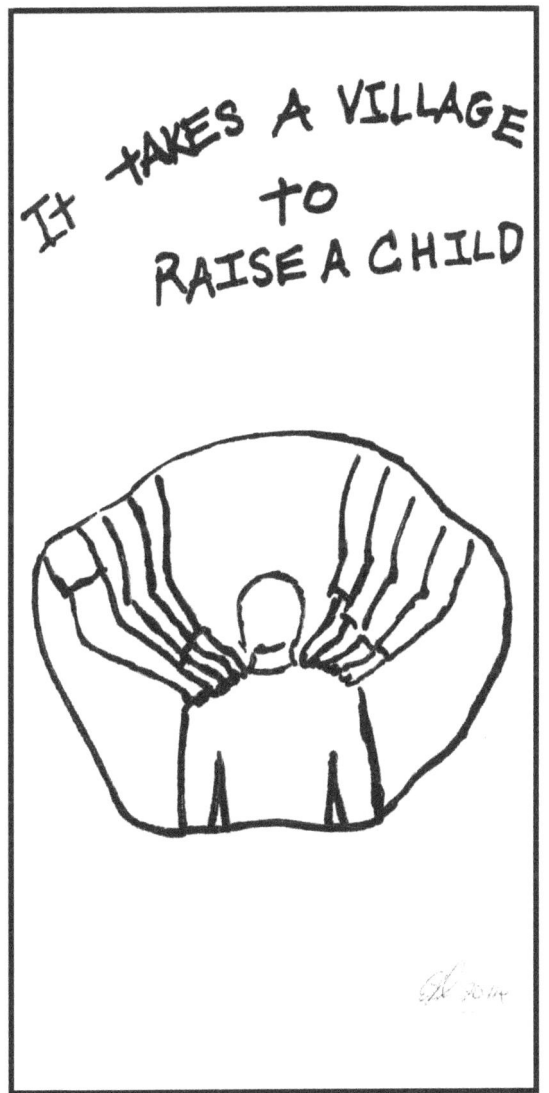

ERIC J. SINGLETON

"Train up a child in the way he should go: and when he is old, he will not depart from it."

Proverbs 22:6

IT TAKES A VILLAGE TO
RAISE A CHILD

Just like all other husbands and wives raising children we had a lot of good times and some not so good times. Several times we have had to tell our children we made mistakes in raising them. We were not perfect then and by no way are we perfect now.

A father and mother can do their very best to instill the right values in their children. Parents try to live in what is said to be the right neighborhood, make sure the children are enrolled in the right school, and make sure they are taken to church. As parents we try to be good listeners, provide financial support, and involve them in extracurricular activities. We provide them with love, patience and understanding, yet in many cases this is not enough.

Years ago when we were children, the village raised the children. The neighbors knew the children and one mother was everyone's mother. There were no problems that the village didn't come together to solve when a child was involved. It could have been something as small as the child using inappropriate language, to skipping school. The neighbors would discipline the child, informing the parent later.

It still takes a village to raise children. The village consists of our parents, neighbors, family, teachers, church members and other adults that children come in contact with on a regular basis. These adults shared the same Christian values.

We know that we do have to be careful; because there are those that will come in with evil intent. That is why we must stay prayed up and just put them in the hands of the Lord. We have to put God first.

I John 2:1, *"My little children, these things write I unto you, that ye sin not. And if any man sin, we have an advocate with the Father, Jesus Christ the righteous."*

Raising children by no means is smooth sailing. My wife and I have gone through numerous situations where our children rebelled and disobeyed us. Our children are adults and it is still a work in process as we are now grandparents. Proverbs 22:6, *"Train up a child in the way he should go: and when he is old, he will not depart from it."*

THANK GOD JUSTICE PREVAILED

ERIC J. SINGLETON

"And let us not be weary in well doing: for in due season we shall reap, if we faint not."

Galatians 6:9

Chapter 6

On May 28, 2007, Memorial Day at approximately 9:00 p.m., a holiday that had been very enjoyable, quiet and peaceful turned into a nightmare.

I was in my "man's room" relaxing and watching the NBA playoffs. My brother and I were calling each other back and forth on the phone. He was at his house, so we were commenting on various plays of the game; something we often did.

One of my sons and his girlfriend came in from another room and informed me that several police officers were outside. Within seconds a police officer was shining a flashlight in the window of the room I was in. I got up, walked to the window and asked the officer what was going on." He said, "Could you come to the front door. I want to talk to you for a minute." I said, "What is this about?" He then told me he would explain when I came to the door. I said, "Okay" and with mixed feelings and curiosity walked to the front door.

When I opened the door I could not believe it! There were sixteen police cars, with over twenty police officers with guns drawn, spotlights and police dogs surrounding our home.

One officer had a blow horn and said very loud, "Put your hands up, come out backwards to the sound of my voice very slowly."

I asked the officer again nervously. "What is this all about?" The officer replied, "Just do what they say, we will get to it." So I did. I went out my front door and three steps down until I reached the center of the driveway. The officer said. "That's far enough", then two officers came over, frisked me, handcuffed me, putting me face down on my lawn. They asked who else was in the house. I answered my wife, son and his girlfriend. I am now getting upset and worried, still asking the officer, "What is this all about" and they are still telling me, "we will get to it."

Meanwhile my wife is in the shower. My son's girlfriend goes and tells her what is going on. She comes out of the shower, grabbing my bathrobe. They come to the front door as well.

The neighbors are now outside watching and the officer on the blow horn calls my son out in the same manner. "You in the white shirt," my son was still holding his keys from the time he came inside informing me the police were outside. My wife told him to keep the keys in his hands and go out the way they called him.

My son's girlfriend was very upset and being a diabetic my wife got her as calm as possible and went out when she was called, "you in the bathrobe."

My wife and son were both put in separate police cars handcuffed. The officer then called my son's girlfriend out in the same manner, handcuffed her and took her across the lawn to the neighbor's tree placing her there with her face toward the tree.

I would love to tell everyone that at that time I thought of God's word. Psalm 23:4, *"Yea, though I walk through the valley of the shadow of death, I will fear no evil: for thou art with me; thy rod and thy staff they comfort me."* I did not at this time, but I did begin praying for our safety, that no one would get hurt.

While we were all handcuffed the officers sent police dogs inside our home to search for I don't know what. One of the officers said, "I know your daughter works at the convenience store down the street and two officers are there," Again, I asked, "What is going on?" and again I was told, "We will get to it."

Meanwhile officers are at my daughter's job where they searched her car only to find nothing. Several moments later the officers came back joining the ones at the house and coming to the conclusion, there is nothing here. After forty-five minutes to an hour they take the handcuffs off all of us. All of the officers leave with the exception of one; he was left to give us an explanation.

Someone had attempted to rob a store down the street and the getaway car was supposed to have matched my daughter's. We later found out that the cars were not a match, one was a two door the other a four door, the color didn't match either. The cars were supposed to have been the same, but we still don't know how accurate that was. The officer apologized for the inconvenience, gave us his card and told us if we had any complaints we could contact his supervisor.

After picking up the police report two days later, we contacted an attorney in our area. He read the report and after a couple of days said that he did not want to go against the police department.

We contacted another attorney, explaining the situation to him over the phone and he said almost the same thing, "I don't want to go against the police department but I wish you well."

No local attorney would touch the case. One of the local attorneys did not want to touch the case but recommended an attorney in Columbia, SC; one hundred and ten miles away from us. I contacted the attorney, he and I instantly connected.

Within a week we were at his Columbia office. Not only did he become our attorney but our friend as well. After more than two years of our attorney coming to Charleston and us going to Columbia whenever needed, working around everyone's busy schedules, for various meetings we finally went to arbitration.

The scripture that comes to mind is Galatians 6:9,*"And let us not be weary in well doing: for in due season we shall reap, if we faint not."*

In due season we finally did reap, even though there were times when I thought I would faint. During arbitration everyone who was involved in that evening were questioned. Stories didn't quite match but God was there, always having a ram in the bush. An older officer told his version of the story and thank God for the ram and thank God for justice. Thank God justice did prevail. This added some much needed closure to this situation.

MY HUMBLE CRY WAS HEARD

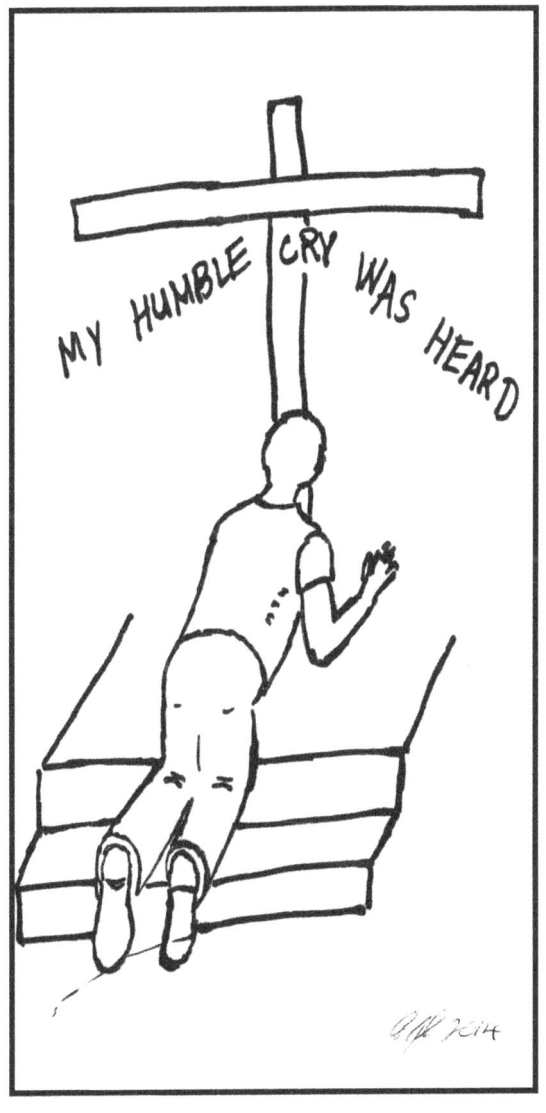

ERIC J. SINGLETON

" Call unto me, and I will answer thee, and show thee great and mighty things, which thou knowest not."

Jeremiah 33:3

Chapter 7

By this time in life, I came out of the family business and my wife closed her child development center. We bought a 40 foot moving truck with double sleepers and began a new venture.

The first ten months we traveled about a 600 mile radius, then a much farther radius averaging 1800 miles. We averaged 2,000 to 3,000 miles of driving per week. I did the driving, and my wife did the paperwork. We both agreed that traveling and being on the road that much, just the two of us brought us closer to each other and even closer to God.

We were back home by most Friday nights or Saturday mornings, just in time to pay the household bills, take care of some things around the house, go to church and visit with family members. Then on Sunday night or Monday morning we were back on the road.

As we traveled the road, we took with us Psalm 27, a familiar hymn.

Verse 1, *"The Lord is my light and my salvation; whom shall I fear? the Lord is the strength of my life; of whom shall I be afraid?"* Verse 5, *"For in the time of trouble he shall hide me in his pavilion: in the secret of his tabernacle shall he hide me; he shall set me up upon a rock."* Verse 14, *"Wait on the Lord: be of good courage, and he shall strengthen thine heart: wait, I say, on the Lord."* I have seen evidence of God's word revealed in each of the verses as we traveled the road.

Traveling back home from Kentucky, we got as far as a truck stop in Rockhill, SC, less than 200 miles from home, that was the night that I believed changed my life forever. I knew we did not need to drive anymore that night, so my wife and I went into the truck stop, took our showers came back to the truck and went to bed. My wife took the top bed and went to sleep right away. I lay down in the bottom bed only a few seconds, sat up and started to panic. All of my thoughts were racing through my mind.

It was 9:00 p.m. on December 23, 2008, I was not praying to God; I was whining and complaining to God. I was spending eleven months on the road, averaging 2-3 thousand miles of driving a week, sometimes more, spending thousands of dollars in truck repairs. Christmas was coming in two days, we still had not finished shopping and did not have the money to but we thought there were things we should buy. I believed Christmas gifts purchases should be cash and carry and not charged.

All of a sudden I heard a loud sound like a tire blowing. I was sitting on the front end of the bottom bed and two feet in front of me appeared a large shadow. Every sound at the truck stop went silent. The large shadow, an image of a man said, "What is the matter son?" I just looked shocked; I looked up at my wife who was still sleeping. A little louder this time the image said, "What's the matter son?" I replied, "Father it seems like the harder I try the tougher things get. Every time I get three steps ahead something happens and knocks me back three steps making it seem as though I'm never getting ahead." He then said, "Son do all you can do, trust in me and I will take care of the rest." I said, "Okay." I looked up at my wife who was still asleep, looked back in front of me and He was gone.

When we got home, within days I was at the church talking with my pastor about the visual experience I had encountered. My pastor told me he was not surprised and told me I should read the book of Jeremiah.

From that the scripture, Jeremiah 33:3 explains my experience, *"Call unto me, and I will answer thee, and show thee great and mighty things, which thou knowest not."*

I believe that I got truly saved that night. I know that everybody does not have that kind of experience but I am grateful that it happened to and for me. From that day forward no matter what the storm, trial, or tribulation I am going through, I know that I can and I must trust in God. I trust God to bring me through and pass the storms providing; I do all that I can and let Him take care of the rest. **Thank God for our Savior.**

It is not about us, we are powerless without God and God gets the glory. Proverbs 27:1, *"Boast not thyself of to morrow; for thou knowest not what a day may bring forth."*

I found out that myself like all others have various learned skills and various God given talents. A lot can be determined by what we do with those skills and talents as in the parables of talents found in Matthew 25:14-30. Even with those skills and talents we should not toot our own horns and think we are in charge. We should remember to do all we can do, trust in God and He will take care of the rest. Stay humble and wait on the Lord.

Praise the Lord, Christmas came and we celebrated. We went to church for worship. We received gifts and brought gifts for friends and family. The gifts may not have been the ones we planned to give but each one was the ones God planned for us to give. After all, whose birthday are we celebrating anyway? It is all about our Lord and

Savior Jesus Christ not us. God's word, John 3:16 says, *"For God so loved the world, that he gave his only begotten Son, that whosoever believeth in him should not perish, but have everlasting life."*

Christmas was a great time to really worship and give praise for the birth of our Lord and Savior Jesus the Christ who gave the gift of life.

After the New Year came in, my entire outlook on life was totally different. Matthew 10:39, *"He that findeth his life shall lose it: and he that loseth his life for my sake shall find it."* God's divine touch had come upon me and I could not take anything for granted anymore. I cannot speak for anyone else but for myself after December 2008, blessings from the Lord came upon me.

The most evidence on a personal level is the urge, desire, even the temptation to use profane language; those four letter words were taken away. That was never my plan, it was God's and I am grateful for it.

A few days after the New Year came in my wife and I left home and were back in our truck, back on the road again. I, with a renewed spirit, no longer measured my success by man's worldly scale but by living a life that is pleasing in God's sight. Psalm 61:5, *"My soul, wait thou only upon God; for my expectation is from Him."*

I would like to say that after that point there were no more struggles, no more trials or tribulations but we all know that is not true. However, when the storms of life do come, I am a lot more at peace because I know who watches over me. Psalm 62:6 God's word, *" He only is my rock and my salvation: he is my defence; I shall not be moved."* In the midst of storms, during the struggles, during the trials and tribulations, I know that if I humble myself and pour out to the Lord, He will hear my cry and answer. Psalm 62:8 says, *"Trust in him at all times; ye people, pour out your heart before him: God is a refuge for us."*

"Wait on the Lord: be of good courage, and he shall strengthen thine heart: wait, I say, on the Lord."

Psalm 27:14

TRAVELING GRACE

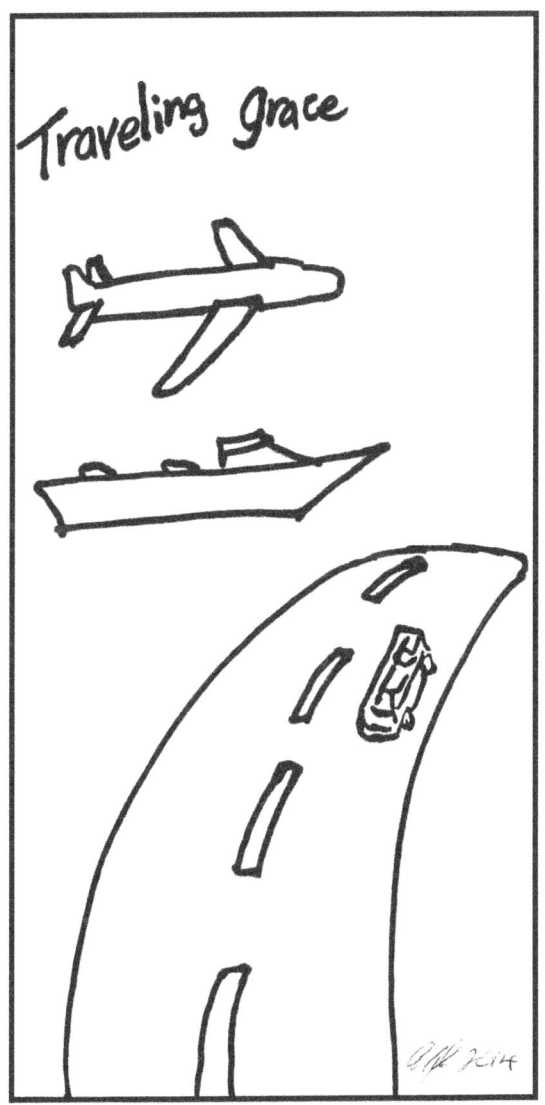

"Six days shalt thou labour, and do all thy work: But the seventh day is the sabbath of the Lord thy God: in it thou shalt not do any work, thou, nor thy son, nor thy daughter, thy manservant, nor thy maidservant, nor thy cattle, nor thy stranger that is within thy gates."

Exodus 20:9-10

Chapter 8

2009 was truly the year, the turning point year that my personal relationship with God grew, becoming a lot stronger. Each week we were still traveling two to three thousand miles a week.

My wife and I had the same weekly goal which was to be home by Friday night or Saturday morning. This way we could be in attendance at our church for Sunday morning worship. God worked it out ninety percent of the time. Romans 12:1 now comes to mind, *"I beseech you therefore, brethren, by the mercies of God, that ye present your bodies a living sacrifice, holy, acceptable unto God, which is your reasonable service."*

We looked forward to leaving town but coming back home was even more rewarding. God's divine touch and presence were definitely upon us. We traveled over one hundred thousand miles in two years, covering thirty-eight out of the fifty states with zero accidents or tickets. It was God's grace and mercy as we traveled.

God kept my wife and me safe on the road but we still had our share of truck breakdowns, once in Fort Hood, Texas at 10:00 p.m. on the interstate. The truck had to be towed to a shop. Another time, we had a breakdown in Florida. A fellow trucker from our company picked us up and took us to the nearest Greyhound bus station. We made a phone call to a truck repair shop in Florida. The truck was towed in as we returned home. After three transfers and seventeen hours later, praise God we were home.

Through all the truck problems, the trials and tribulation on the road God always put very kind and helpful people in our paths during our times of need. God's word, Job 11:18, *"And thou shalt be secure, because there is hope; yea, thou shalt dig about thee, and thou shalt take thy rest in safety."*

We traveled all over the east coast, from the Florida Keys to Buffalo, NY, then to the Midwest, Denver, Colorado to New Mexico working and coming home on the weekend to Charleston, SC. We traveled constantly for eleven months.

My wife planned a cruise for us in November. When November came we had two more pick ups to make both in West Palm Beach, Florida. I remembered it like it was yesterday. We picked up one shipment, the second one the next day. We have family that lives in West Palm Beach, Florida so we called them. We told them we were in town, so we went over and fellowshipped with them. We left out the next morning, heading for home.

Everything worked out because I believe God was in the midst. The shipments for New Jersey and Boston, Massachusetts did not have to be delivered. So, as soon as we got home we were off for a one week vacation. We were tired and ready for rest and relaxation. Matthew 11:28, Jesus said, *"Come unto me, all ye that labour and are heavy laden, and I will give you rest."* ("No test, No testimony").

When we got on that cruise ship I was relieved because I did not feel like I ran away from my responsibilities but it was very nice to put them on hold. All but one, I could not put on hold. The more I tried to relax, the more that one responsibility kept poking at me. It was time for a change. I told my wife while sitting beside the pool. "I cannot do this anymore." She asked, "Can't do what anymore?" I told her I could not be a long distance truck driver anymore. She reminded me that we still had two shipments that needed to be delivered. I said to her, "I can't even deliver those."

As soon as I confessed that decision I was totally at peace from that moment on. For the remainder of the cruise I was totally at peace. My wife probably thought I had lost my mind, but I was being led by the spirit for quite a while. Working from early in the morning until late at night and sometimes into the next morning, I knew it was time to stop. Psalm 34:15-17. *"The eyes of the Lord are upon the righteous, and his ears are open unto their cry. The face of the Lord is against them that do evil, to cut off the remembrance of them from the earth. The righteous cry, and the Lord heareth, and delivereth them out of all their troubles."*

I wish I could say that I was financially secured and had time to look for a great job but that would be far from the truth. The truth is I was in serious financial trouble, behind in most of the bills.

Within a few days I was employed at a local car wash making minimum wages; working six days a week,

Monday-Saturday at fifty years old. I was grateful to God to have a job. Most of my co-workers were half my age or younger, but I did not care about that. God gave me an opportunity, a very humbling opportunity and I was going to take full advantage of it.

God's word kept me going. Exodus 20:9-10 states: *"Six days shalt thou labour, and do all thy work: But the seventh day is the sabbath of the Lord thy God: in it thou shalt not do any work, thou, nor thy son, nor thy daughter, thy manservant, nor thy maidservant, nor thy cattle, nor thy stranger that is within thy gates."*

We all need a day to worship, to heal physically and or mentally from our labor. We all need a day of rest and time to spend with our family. Exodus

20:11 states: *"For in six days the Lord made heaven and earth, the sea, and all that in them is, and rested the seventh day: wherefore the Lord blessed the sabbath day, and hallowed it."*

Like most believers, I believe you can and should worship God anywhere and everywhere everyday but there is something about going into God's house (the church) and being with other worshippers. There is strength in numbers good or bad. Most people would prefer strength in good numbers. Psalm 95:6-7, *"O come, let <u>us</u> worship and bow down: let <u>us</u> kneel before the Lord <u>our</u> maker. For He is <u>our</u> God; and <u>we</u> are the people of His pasture, and the sheep of His hand. To day if ye will hear his voice ."* If you are at home or anywhere else outside of the church, I don't know if a person can receive the spiritual armor to deal with the outside world's satanic and demonic forces and temptations. We all battle temptations every day in one way or another.

HUMBLING PERIODS AND GROWING PAINS

"Be not rash with thy mouth, and let not thine heart be hasty to utter any thing before God: for God is in heaven, and thou upon earth: therefore let thy words be few."

Ecclesiastes 5:2

HUMBLING PERIODS AND GROWING PAINS

Chapter 9

I thought that I would probably be at the car wash for a month or two, but it was considerably longer. I was at the car wash for nine months. Being at the car wash for nine months did not cause me to be bitter, I got better. Better at having more compassion for other people. People who were really struggling financially because I was one of them.

At the same time I knew in my spirit God was calling me to be a spiritual leader, so when the pastor and the chairman of the deacon's ministry called me. I knew God was in control. So, despite my financial circumstances the time had come to become one of God's humble servants. I considered myself blessed and honored to serve in this capacity.

My nine months of deacon in training period began. My wife as my support began deaconess training; this was nine months as well. Proverbs 18:22, *"Whoso findeth a wife findeth a good thing, and obtaineth favour of the Lord."* The Bible also says in Genesis

HUMBLING PERIODS AND GROWING PAINS

2:18, *" And the Lord God said, It is not good that the man should be alone; I will make him an help meet for him."* The deaconess (the wife) is a help meet, to help and support the deacon (the husband).

I would love to say that after I had accepted the calling from God all or most of my trials and tribulations went away, but we all know that is not the case. I was still working at the car wash six days a week and hauling steel and scrap metal whenever I could or whenever it rained or the car wash was closed. I did whatever I had to do that was legal to pay the mortgage and household bills. Once again, God's word would come in my mind during tough times and struggles. Galatians 6:9, *"And let us not be weary in well doing: for in due season we shall reap, if we faint not."* That scripture is deeply embedded in my heart and it keeps me going during tough and challenging times.

God hears prayers and God hears when we praise his name. For a very long period in my life, well into adult hood and even as a married man with children, whenever I prayed to God I was asking Him for something either for my family or myself. This was probably ninety percent of my prayers.

Today, I praise God's name morning, noon, evening and night. My prayers today are quite the opposite of what it used to be. Probably, ninety percent of my prayers now are giving thanks for what He has done, for what

He is doing, and for what He is going to do in my life. Now, I count my blessings and not my problems. God's word says in II Corinthians 5:7, *"For we walk by faith, not by sight."* With that scripture (God's Word) truly believing that in my heart, (faith) and keeping my hands in God's unchanging hands (work) I am certain that everything is going to be alright. Because Faith without works is dead.

In 2010, one week before I became an ordained deacon, I received a call from a job search agency informing me that a local CDL truck driving position had become available for me. Praise God! I put in my notice at the car wash and the following week I was on my new job.

I left the car wash on good terms, thankful and humbled for the opportunity. Ecclesiastes 5:2, *"Be not rash with thy mouth, and let not thine heart be hasty to utter any thing before God: for God is in heaven, and thou upon earth: therefore let thy words be few."*

At first adjusting to a different work pace was challenging. But I knew I would adjust because trucking was something I did my entire adult life. God sent a better opportunity for me to take a little better care of my family and me. Ecclesiastes 5:12, *"The sleep of a labouring man is sweet, whether he eat little or much: but the abundance of the rich will not suffer him to sleep."*

During those adjusting period years, to stay afloat financially I borrowed money which is only a temporary quick fix; I learned that the hard way. I am slowly but surely paying it all back which is not easy but is personally satisfying and rewarding. Proverbs 22:7 says, *"The rich ruleth over the poor, and the borrower is servant to the lender."* I feel that I have been the borrower and the servant to the lender long enough. Therefore, I never financed luxury only necessities if I absolutely had to. I was never a person that spent money foolishly, but I believe now in learning to live on less than what I make. It does take obedience but it is well worth it. Isaiah 1:19-20 says, *"If ye be willing and obedient, ye shall eat the good of the land: But if ye refuse and*

rebel, ye shall be devoured with the sword: for the mouth of the Lord hath spoken it."
Thank God for second chances!

So many hardships that most of us have encountered could so easily have been avoided if we only trust in God's word for everything and not the world's way. Listening to our elders that have and are living a life obedient to God's word would not have hurt either. Sometimes we are given Godly advice and just don't listen because we are living by sight. Now having four adult children (three sons and one daughter) my wife and I realize that we made many mistakes. Just like many other parents some bad choices were made and we have regrets; none of us are perfect. We cannot erase whatever was

HUMBLING PERIODS AND GROWING PAINS

done or not done in our lives, but because God is a God of second chances, we all have an opportunity to be forgiven for our sins and saved from our sins. God's words says in Romans 10:9, *"That if thou shalt confess with thy mouth the Lord Jesus, and shalt believe in thine heart that God hath raised him from the dead, thou shalt be saved."*

It is never too early in life or never too late in life to want to be saved. None of us know when we are going to die, but we need to be ready. Being saved is our only way to eternal life and our only way to live a complete and happy life. A life that is pleasing in God's sight here on earth. God's word, John 3:16, *"For God so loved the world, that he gave his only begotten Son, that whosoever believeth in him should not perish, but have everlasting life."*

Most adults with children are very concerned about their children's safety, their relationships, and their careers. My wife and I are no different, we are concerned about all those areas in our children's lives as well. We were concerned when they were children, teenagers and now even more so as they are adults. We pray for our children every day. We pray that they will make the right decisions. We pray that each of them will have a personal relationship with God and their souls be saved. We also pray that while they are going through relationships, struggles, trials and financial challenges they do

HUMBLING PERIODS AND GROWING PAINS

not fall victims to the negative strongholds of the word.

At times it seems like our adult children have a different value system. I know there are a lot of other people with adult children who feel the same way. But we must remember God's words, Proverbs 22: 6, *"Train up a child in the way he should go: and when he is old, he will not depart from it."* Three out of our four children have children of their own. I know that they want the best for their children just like we wanted the best for them.

Raising children, working spouses setting aside date nights, and most importantly worshiping God in a lifestyle that is pleasing in His sight may sometimes seem like one great big juggling act; they are all needed and they are all necessary. As soon as I started counting only my blessings and stopped counting my problems life's whole juggling act has become so much easier.

In Proverbs 8:33-34 it says, *"Hear instruction, and be wise, and refuse it not. Blessed is the man that heareth me, watching daily at my gates, waiting at the posts of my doors."* God's word gives me the strength to continue when I get tired, discouraged and feel like throwing in the towel.

I normally go to bed at night and sleep straight through. However about

HUMBLING PERIODS AND GROWING PAINS

once or twice a month I would go to sleep and wake up within an hour or so feeling like the entire world's pressures were on my shoulders. When this would happen in the past I tossed and turned all night. Now, that I know God and His word that says in Matthew 11:28, Jesus speaking, *"Come unto me, all ye that labour and are heavy laden, and I will give you rest."* So now on those nights I get up, find a quiet place where I can meet God, pray and read His words and listen to Him. Upon returning in bed I can then have a restful night.

This has become habit, I know everything is a process, good habits as well as bad ones. In life we are better at establishing and working on good habits. If you did not grow up going to church, make a decision to go. Find a good Bible based church where you can feel the Holy Spirit and begin a relationship with God. A church where the members show a true Christ like love towards each other. With love in your own heart to give you will receive love in return.

I know when someone does something wrong to us or say something to offend or embarrass us, our first response is to retaliate if we are living in the flesh. However, if we are living in the spirit, yes, we may still be tempted to react in the flesh and retaliate; but when we think about what

HUMBLING PERIODS AND GROWING PAINS

Jesus would do or if the way we want to act would be pleasing to God we would respond differently.

God's word, Leviticus 19:18, *"Thou shalt not avenge, nor bear any grudge against the children of thy people, but thou shalt love thy neighbour as thyself: I am the Lord."*

The more we study the word of God and the more we keep our hands in God's unchanging spiritual hands the easier it becomes to love thy neighbor as thyself even when our neighbor is not very loveable.

Psalm 1:1 says, *"Blessed is the man that walketh not in the counsel of the ungodly, nor standeth in the way of sinners, nor sitteth in the seat of the scornful."*

Living a blessed life with my wife, having raised our children to the best of our ability, I now realize it could have been much easier. However, like so many other people I believed in God but I did not seek God for myself. I did not study God's word (the Bible) for myself. Psalm 34:12, 15 and 17, *"What man is he that desireth life, and loveth many days, that he may see good? The eyes of the Lord are upon the righteous, and his ears are open unto their cry. The righteous cry, and the Lord heareth, and delivereth them out of all their troubles."*

I can only speak for myself, but I believe that if I had read Psalm 1:1 paid attention to it, believed it in my heart and made it my way of life a long time ago, I could have been much further along in life, both spiritually and financially. I would not have made as many mistakes as I did in life. I did a lot of wrong things on purpose knowing it was wrong because I wanted to fit in and be accepted by a certain group of people that did not have my best interest at heart.

I know I am not alone when I say that I may be one of the few people willing to admit that I knowingly did wrong things. I hope any and everyone who reads this will realize that they are blessed and make a decision not to follow the ungodly. This would be a life changing decision because it would prevent a lot of heartache and pain!

"If ye be willing and obedient, ye shall eat the good of the land: But if ye refuse and rebel, ye shall be devoured with the sword: for the mouth of the Lord hath spoken it."

Isaiah 1:19-20

CALL ON THE HEALER FIRST, THEN CALL THE DOCTOR SECOND

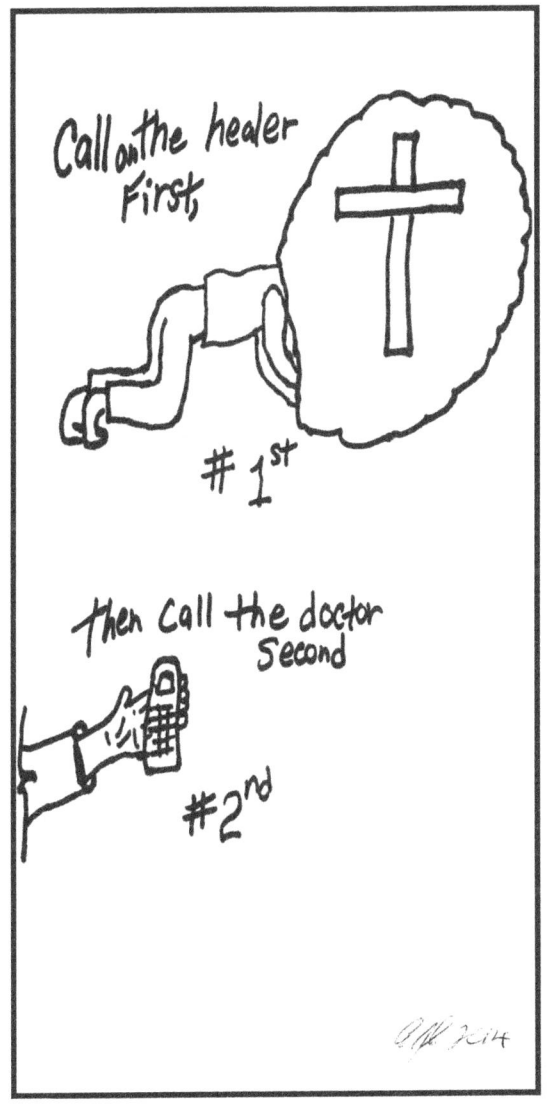

"He that hath an ear, let him hear what the Spirit saith unto the churches; To him that overcometh will I give to eat of the tree of life, which is in the midst of the paradise of God."

Revelation 2:7

CALL ON THE HEALER FIRST, THEN CALL THE DOCTOR SECOND

Jeremiah 33:3, *"Call unto me, and I will answer thee, and show thee great and mighty things, which thou knowest not."* I know that had I called on the Lord instead of others for so many years in so many situations a lot of my hardships as well as a stomach ulcer

would have probably been avoided, but thank God for God.

I believe that due to my faith, God showed me favor, and to my doctor's surprise when I went back to him for a three months check-up my ulcer was healed. To God be the Glory! The doctor and medication did not heal my ulcer. It was the Healer, the Master, my Lord and Savior Jesus Christ. Psalm 6:2, *"Have mercy upon me, O Lord; for I am weak: O Lord, heal me; for my bones are vexed."* Psalm 103:3, *"Who forgiveth all thine iniquities; who healeth all thy diseases."* Matthew 9:35, *"And Jesus went about all the cities and villages, teaching in their synagogues, and preaching the gospel of the kingdom, and healing every sickness and every disease among the people."*

CALL ON THE HEALER FIRST, THEN CALL THE DOCTOR SECOND

We should listen to our bodies especially as we get older, exercise, eat properly, get our medical checkups when needed but especially have a listening ear to our Father which is in Heaven. Revelation 2:7, *"He that hath an ear, let him hear what the Spirit saith unto the churches; To him that overcometh will I give to eat of the tree of life, which is in the midst of the paradise of God."* I thank God every morning when I wake for what He has done in my life, for what He is doing in my life and for what He is going to do in my life. I Corinthians 1:9, *"God is faithful, by whom ye were called unto the fellowship of his Son Jesus Christ our Lord."*

Just as we have learned through life to plan and prepare for a test at school, sports, jobs, vacations, marriages, children, etc.; which is all good, it is only temporary. I believe the most and biggest decision we will have to make on this earth, is the decision of salvation. Where will you spend eternity? Heaven or hell!! It is just a decision, but an important one. Romans 10:9, *"That if thou shalt confess with thy mouth the Lord Jesus, and shalt believe in thine heart that God hath raised him from the dead, thou shalt be saved."* Romans 10:10, *"For with the heart man believeth unto righteousness; and with the mouth confession is made unto salvation."*

CALL ON THE HEALER FIRST, THEN CALL THE DOCTOR SECOND

"Eternal life, it is just a decision."

A good Bible based church on a weekly basis is an excellent idea.

God Bless!

"Have mercy upon me,

O Lord; for I am weak:

O Lord, heal me; for my

bones are vexed."

Psalm 6:2

www.ingramcontent.com/pod-product-compliance
Lightning Source LLC
Chambersburg PA
CBHW071719040426
42446CB00011B/2131